Send a Note Today!

By

Ana Navarra

authorHOUSE™

1663 LIBERTY DRIVE, SUITE 200
BLOOMINGTON, INDIANA 47403
(800) 839-8640
WWW.AUTHORHOUSE.COM

First published by AuthorHouse 08/31/04

ISBN: 1-4184-9036-9 (sc)

Library of Congress Control Number: 2004096059

Printed in the United States of America
Bloomington, Indiana

This book is printed on acid-free paper.

TABLE OF CONTENTS

ANNIVERSARIES

* I love you to Infinity plus ONE! Happy Anniversary.

* Thank you for all our Yesterdays, Todays and every sweet Tomorrow. Happy Anniversary!

* To a perfectly matched couple. Happy Anniversary!

* Remember that communication is everything. Happy Anniversary with love and hugs.

* Wishing you a wonderful day. Happy Anniversary!

* Nothing is impossible when I am with you. Happy Anniversary and many more!

* Today is very special because you are! Happy Anniversary.

* Best Wishes to you for a very Happy Anniversary.

* Happy Anniversary to you Both from Both of us!

* The Special joys of sharing life together. May these be yours today and every day. Happy Anniversary.

* To a very special couple celebrating a very special love. Happy Anniversary.

* Every time I look at you, I think about how much I love you. That is why I'm always looking at you. Happy Anniversary.

* Thank you for loving me just the way I am. Happy Anniversary!

* May the love of today be ever lasting. Happy Anniversary!

* May the love of this day be captured in your hearts for the many years to come. Happy Anniversary!

* I love you with all my heart! Happy Anniversary.

* When I am around you, I'm a little Bolder, a little Braver, a little Sillier and a whole lot happier. Happy Anniversary!

* Happy Anniversary with love to a wonderful couple.

* Happy Anniversary to our favorite couple!

* Best Wishes for a special couple.

* Anniversaries are for making memories of happy times. Happy Anniversary.

* You are the best thing that ever happened to me. Happy Anniversary.

* We are thinking of you today and always. Happy Anniversary.

* Wishing you another year filled with happiness and joy.

* You are the special kind of couple who is always remembered. Happy Anniversary.

BIRTHDAYS

* Wishing you a happy day with special moments to enjoy and remember. Happy Birthday!

* For a Special Friend. Far brighter than sunshine and sweeter than roses are the many good wishes this greeting discloses. Happy Birthday!

* For a Special Friend. For someone too nice to forget on a very special day. Happy Birthday!

* Hope your birthday brings you happiness in everything you do, for today's a celebration of a special person….. YOU!

* On your birthday and everyday, may you enjoy all the beautiful things life has to offer. Happy Birthday!

* Happy Birthday! Eat Cake and Enjoy Your Day.

* It's Your Birthday, Have a Perfect Day!

* Wishing you a very special day filled with much joy and happiness.

* Birthday Blessings; May the good lord grant you happiness…..and may He always fill your life with grace and peace. Happy Birthday!

* Wishing you everything that will make your birthday and the coming year a happy one. Happy Birthday!

* Wishing a Very Special Friend a Very Special Happy Birthday!

* Happy Birthday to a very special Person!

* Wishing you a special day filled with fun and love. Happy Birthday!

* A Very Happy Birthday To You and Many Many More!

* Wishing a special friend the happiest of birthdays, Enjoy your day!

* A Birthday Prayer; Today and always, may God's gift of love be yours. Happy Birthday!

* Hope your birthdays will always be filled with lots of fun and lots of friends to share with! Happy Birthday!

* Your Birthday? MAGNIFICO! Have a happy one.

* Happy Birthday to a chic chick!

* Reach for a star.... It's your birthday all over the world!

* Your age is the cool age to be!

* I thought for once I'd get you a nice birthday card, One that doesn't remind you of how damn old you are! Happy Birthday!

* Happy Birthday! May all your dreams come true.

* You are my sunshine! Happy Birthday.

* Don't think of it as getting older; just think of it as going on ahead to check things out for the rest of us! Happy Birthday.

* Happy Birthday to my favorite and only sister and remember that the key to a great birthday is to lie back and enjoy it. Happy Birthday!

* Enjoy the simple gifts of every day. It's your birthday, Relax like crazy!

* No fancy words or phrases, just a few lines to say I hope you spend your birthday in your very favorite way. Happy Birthday!

* Wishing you a sunny smile, a cheerful heart and a perfect day. Happy Birthday!

* May this birthday be one you'll remember again and again with happiness.

* You're off to another wonderful year. Happy Birthday!

* Picked the best wish I could find…. For it was picked with you in mind. Have a Happy Birthday!

* Celebrate your birthday in style!

* It's your birthday; Run, Laugh, Dance and play… have a glorious day!

* Happy Birthday to a glamour girl!

* To know you is to wish you happiness. Happy Birthday!

* Make a big deal out of birthdays, Especially yours!

* A wish is a gift the heart makes. Today you are wished a Happy Birthday from my heart!

* Hooray for you! Happy B'Day!

* Me? Forget your birthday? I don't think so! Hope is happy.

* Celebrate, Celebrate, Celebrate! Happy Birthday!

* May the year to come be all that you hope for. Happy Birthday!

* Wishing you all the happiness your special day can hold! Happy Birthday!

* Dress up for the occasion, It is Your Birthday!

* What a special time for you! Happy Birthday

* Party Time! Happy Birthday!

* Wishing you all the things you're dreaming of will come true. Happy Birthday!

* Take time to smell the roses and have a happy birthday!

* It's your birthday.... Pamper yourself!

* Dance, Sing and Dream, it's your birthday!

* Hope your birthday makes you happy all over!

* Surprise! I remembered your birthday!

* Birthday Rules: Stay Cute, Wish Big and Never let anyone count your candles. Happy Day!

Ana Navarra

*   Happy Birthday from a big fan of yours.

*   ¡FELIZ CUMPLEAÑOS!

CHRISTMAS

* Rejoice in the spirit of Christmas, which is Peace, the miracle of Christmas, which is Hope, and the heart of Christmas, which is Love. Merry Christmas.

* May the harmony of the season live in your heart this Christmas.

* May the joy and peace of this blessed season be with you now and in the New Year!

* Wishing you a blessed Christmas and joyous New Year.

* Wishing you warmth and good cheer this holiday season.

* May all your holiday dreams come true. Merry Christmas!

* Wishing you the beauty of the season.

* Season Greetings!

* Peace On Earth!

* May all the joy you give away…. Return to you on Christmas Day!

* Merry Christmas! Happy New Year!

* Joy to the world and specially to you. Merry Christmas!

* Rejoice! Celebrate its Christmas time!

* Hope your holidays are bright with surprise and delight.

* Happy Holidays! Wishing you a bright and Merry Christmas!

* Wishing you all the joy and magic of this holiday season. Merry Christmas!

* ¡FELIZ NAVIDAD!

* Happy Holidays and a Prosperous New Year.

* Peace and Love around the world, It's Christmas time!

EASTER

*   The special joys of sharing life together. May these be yours today and every day. Happy Easter!

*   HAPPY EASTER TO YOU!

*   Easter Greetings with love.

*   Happy Easter, Happy Spring to you all!

*   May your Easter be filled with wonderful surprises. Have a Happy Day!

*   Easter is the time to remember to Live, Love and Hope. Happy Easter.

*   Easter is a time to reflect on the wonder and beauty life can bring. Wishing you Easter Blessings.

*   Sending you warm wishes for a Happy Easter!

*   We will be thinking of you on Easter!

* May friendship, love and happiness fill your home this holiday. Happy Easter!

* Happiness is where you find it. Find it this Easter!

* Easter is a time to be thankful for family, friends and health.

* In the spirit of Easter, we wish you a happy holiday!

* For Someone Special on Easter. You help make our family a hoppy one! Happy Easter!!!

* Easter is in the Air. Best Easter Wishes!

* HAPPY EASTER!

* Have a groovy day. Happy Easter!

* Easter is coming, Hop yours is Hoppy!

* Wishing you the best for a season of sunshine and joy. Happy Easter!

*   An Easter 'Hello' and a special wish too, may springtime be wonderfully happy for you!

*   Spring has hatched! Happy Easter.

*   Sending you bright and happy wishes for a Happy Easter!

FATHER'S DAY

* Wishing a Happy Father's Day to a real Dad!

* This card was made Especially For You!

* Dad, you were born to be wild!

* You are the best Dad Ever. Happy Father's Day!

* The best part of all is just knowing you are there. Thanks Dad. Happy Father's Day.

* Wishing you a great big happy father's Day!

* Having a father like you is one of the most beautiful things in life.

* Love to you on Father's Day and always.

* May this day be one you'll remember again and again with happiness. Happy Father's Day

* You're loved today and all year through! Happy Father's Day!

*   You deserve every happiness today! Happy Father's Day.

*   To know you is to love you Dad!

*   A wish is a gift the heart makes. Today you are wished a day filled with all the joy a day can bring, all the love a heart can hold and all the happiness you so deserve. Happy Father's Day.

*   For someone special, a special wish for Father's Day!

*   Hope you have a day that's happy through and through because there couldn't ever be a day too nice for you. Happy Father's Day!

*   It's your Special Day! You're a Special Dad!

*   Dad fish a happy day for you today!

*   Thinking of you Today. Happy Father's Day!

*   Dad kick back and enjoy your day!

*   Dad your influence is all over us, Happy Father's Day!

*   Thank you for sowing the seeds of love Dad!

*   Salud! Here is to you and all you do. Happy Father's Day!

*   Thank you Dad for leading by example. Much love to you today and always.

*   Dad this card is not big enough to fit the medal you deserve. Happy Father's Day!

GRADUATION

* Congratulations! You Did It!

* Wishing you dreams to dream, a song to sing and the very best of everything.

* Reach out for the stars! Congratulations to a star catcher.

* Make a wish….. You graduated!

* Happy Graduation. Congratulations!

* Congratulations Graduate!

* U R A star! Congrats.

* Congratulations on your accomplishment and dedication!

* It's over! Celebrate! Scream! Dream and Dance! Congratulations.

* Have a groovy Graduation Day!

* Wishing you the moon and the stars. Congratulations Graduate!

* May this day be one you'll remember again and again with pride. Congratulations.

* May the years to come be all that you hope for. Congratulations!

* Wishing you every happiness today and always. Happy Graduation Day!

* May all your wishes and dreams come true.

* Salud! Cheers! To the Graduate!

* Congratz! You did it.

* May all our wishes, dreams and job offers for you come true.

HALLOWEEN

* This Halloween, I vant to nibble your kibble.

* You're my little Halloween Witch!

* Beware of black cats and tall pointy hats. Happy Halloween!

* I LOVE YOU! Happy Halloween.

* We be Bad, hope Your Halloween Be Good!

* BOO!!!! Happy Halloween.

* BOO!!! Hope your Halloween is simply spook-tacular!

* I LOVE YOU! On Halloween and Always!

* Watch out for whatever will cross your path today..... Happy Halloween!

* Happy Halloween Cover Ghoul!

* Halloween fashions: Blue eye shadow with green skin.

* Make mortals suffer! Happy Halloween!

* Warts are in! Happy Halloween!

* Because you're so special and loved a whole lot too, on Halloween is fun to make this great big wish for you, Happy Halloween!

* May you enjoy the special delights of this glorious scary night. Happy Halloween!

* Wishing you a Scary, Scary Night! Happy Halloween!

* Have a frightfully good and fun Halloween!

* Hope your Halloween is a howler!

* Witch you were here!

* Wishing you a day full of tricks and treats.

* May sweet little pleasures bring lots of happiness to you today.

INSPIRATIONAL

* Nothing splendid has ever been achieved except by those who dared believe that something inside of them was superior to circumstance. – John Barton

* The best way to succeed in life is to act on the advice we give others. – Anon

* With courage you will dare to take risks, have the strength to be compassionate and the wisdom to be humble. Courage is the foundation of integrity. – Keshavan Nair

* To gain that which is worth having, it may be necessary to lose everything else. – Bernadette Devlin

* The questions which one asks oneself begin, at last, to illuminate the world. – James Baldwin

* Few will have the greatness to bend history itself, but each of us can work to change a small portion of events. – Robert Kennedy

* Insist on yourself never imitate. – Emerson

* Look within. Within is the fountain of good, and it will even bubble up, if thou wilt ever dig. – Marcus Aurelius

* If I am not I, who will be? – Thoreau

* Good people are good because they come to wisdom through failure. – William Saroyan

* We must become the change we want to see. – Gandhi

* Never fear being vulgar, just boring. – Diana Vreeland

* Everyone has been made for some particular work and the desire for that work has been put in his or her heart. – Rumi

* If you think you can or you think you can't, you are right. – Henry Ford

* A man is happy so long as he chooses to be happy and nothing can stop him. – Alexander Solzhenitsyn

* Ring the bells that still can ring, Forget your perfect offering, There is a crack in everything, That's how the light gets in. – Leonard Cohen

* This is a world of action, and not for moping and groaning in. – Charles Dickens

* One must still have chaos in oneself to be able to give birth to a dancing star. – Fredrich Nietzsche

* It is by will alone that I set my mind in motion. – Memtat Prayer

* Trust in yourself. Your perceptions are often more accurate than you are willing to believe. – Claudia Black

* There is a bit of magic in everything, and some loss to even things out. – Lou Reed

* We are all in the gutter, but some of us are looking at the stars. – Oscar Wilde

* Believe nothing, no matter where you read it or who has said it, not even if I have said it, unless it agrees with your own reason and your own common sense. – Buddha

* May You Live all the days of your life – Jonathan Swift

* May good luck be your friend in whatever you do, and may trouble be always a stranger to you.

* May you have all the happiness and luck that life can hold - And at the end of all your rainbows may you find a pot of gold.

MOTHER'S DAY

* You have all the essentials that make a great MOM. Happy Mother's Day.

* The world would be a better place with more Mother's like you. Happy Mother's Day!

* I love you for all you do for all of us. Happy Mother's Day!

* For My Aunt, Wishing you a Mother's Day that's as wonderful and fun as you! XOXO

* May sweet little pleasures bring you happiness today. Happy Mother's Day!

* Today you are wished a day filled with all the joy a day can bring, all the love a heart can hold and all the happiness you so deserve. Happy Mother's Day!

* Happy Mother's Day to the one who cares the most about me.

* Happy Mother's Day, I love you!

* Pamper yourself, It's Mother's Day!

* Laugh, Cry, Dance, Play and Nag, do whatever makes you happy, It is Mother's Day!

* Sending you bright and happy wishes for a Special Mother's Day!

* Hope your day is as special as you are! Happy Mother's Day!

* You are a star today, pamper yourself and shine! Happy Mother's Day!

* Hope you feel like the queen of all that surrounds you! Happy Mother's Day!

* To a special Daughter, Mother and Wife with love. Happy Mother's Day!

* Because you are such a special Mother and loved a whole lot too, On Mother's Day it's fun to make this great big wish for you! Happy Mother's Day!

*   Here's a warm Mother's Day wish for you because you're loved a lot today and all year through. Happy Mother's Day!

*   May this day be one you'll remember again and again with happiness. Happy Mother's Day!

*   Happy Mother's Day to the one who makes me happy all over.

*   You deserve the very best today and always! Happy Mother's Day.

*   Wishing you a Mother's Day that's as cheerful and fun as you! XOXO

*   You are an inspiration to me. Happy Mother's Day!

NEW HOME

* May the light always dance in your eyes, and laughter brighten your smile. May peace prevail at your hearth and love always welcome your home. Congratulations on your New Home.

* May your home be always cozy and a reflection of the two of you. Congratulations!

* Enjoy your home today and always.

* May your home be filled with bunches of love and bouquets of happiness.

* Make your home where your dreams will grow and a world to match your dreams.

* May your home bring you an extra measure of good fortune.

* Make sure friendship, health, love and success fill your New Home Always.

* May your troubles be less and your blessings be more. And nothing but happiness come through your door.

* May your home be filled with laughter, May your pockets be filled with gold, And may you have all the happiness Your Irish heart can hold.

SYMPATHY

* May you find comfort with your loved ones in this time of sorrow.

* So very sorry for your loss.

* With Deepest Sympathy.

* Know that we mourn with you in this time of sadness.

* Thinking of you now and always.

* Make your memories and faith carry you through this time of sorrow.

* May today be the celebration of a new life.

* May the memories fill your heart with lasting warmth and joy.

THANK YOU

* Thank you for loving me just the way I am!

* To thoughtful you from thankful me!

* Thank you for all our Yesterdays, Todays and every sweet Tomorrow.

* It is easy to say Thank You, but it's harder to convey the deep and heart felt gratitude I really feel today. But maybe having said this much by now I've let you know your thoughtfulness means more to me than words will ever show.

* Thank you for the lovely gift and for all your kindness.

* Thank you for being an inspiration to us and for being such a positive influence in our life. We would've never done it without you. Thank you! Thank you!

* You are my hero and inspiration, thank you.

* You are my reason for smiling, thank you again and again!

* Thinking of your kindness and sending you many thanks!

* Thank you. My gratitude is immense!

* Thank you very much. You are the Best.

* It's in your nature to be so thoughtful. Thank you from us all!

* Thank you for being our friend and making our day extra special.

* Just wanted to say, "THANK YOU"

* THANK YOU! For the food, fun and friends. "There is more to life than increasing its speed – Gandhi"

* Thank you for the wonderful surprise.

* Thanks from the bottom of my heart for all you do for me.

*   Thank you for going out of your way to make time for me.

*   Thank you for giving so freely.

*   Your thoughts put my mind at ease, Thank you!

*   Thank you for being the kind and generous person that you are.

*   Thank you for always knowing just how to make others feel cared for and loved.

*   THANK YOU for being you!

*   With heartfelt, Thanks!

THANKSGIVING

* HAPPY THANKSGIVING TO YOU!

* Best Thanksgiving Wishes from all of us.

* It's a beautiful time of year to give thanks for all we have. Happy Thanksgiving!

* Thanksgiving makes me think of all the blessings in my life and that includes you! Happy Thanksgiving with love.

* The special joys of sharing life together. May these be yours today and every day. Happy Thanksgiving!

* Happy Thanksgiving Greetings with love.

* Happy Thanksgiving from our home to yours.

* May your Thanksgiving be filled with wonderful surprises. Have a Happy Day!

* Thanksgiving is the time to remember to Live, Love and Hope. Happy Thanksgiving.

* Thanksgiving is a time to reflect on the wonder and beauty life can bring. Wishing you a very Happy Thanksgiving.

* Sending you warm wishes for a Happy Thanksgiving!

* We will be thinking of you on Thanksgiving!

* May friendship, family, love and happiness fill your home this holiday. Happy Thanksgiving!

* Happiness is where you find it, Happy Thanksgiving!

* Thanksgiving is a time to be thankful for family, friends and health. Happy Thanksgiving with Love!

* In the spirit of Thanksgiving, we wish you a happy holiday!

* During this time of Thanksgiving, Thank you.

* At Thanksgiving and always, never forget....you're never forgotten!

* I give thanks today for all my yesterdays because they led me to you. Happy Thanksgiving to the one I love!

* Just for you. Today and always we are thankful for you. Happy Thanksgiving.

* Wishing you the best of the season and a very Happy Thanksgiving.

* Warmest wishes to you for a very happy Thanksgiving.

THINKING OF YOU

*   May your joys be many. Just thinking of you today.

*   May you have a long life full of happiness and health.

*   I just wanted to let you know that I often think of you. Best Wishes to you today and always for all you have done for me.

*   Only letting you know that you are in my thoughts often. XO XO

*   Just wanted to let you know someone somewhere is thinking of you today.

*   Do you know that I admire you for your strength, courage and so much more? Now you do.

*   I want to grow up to be like you!

*   A friend always remembers a friend. Thinking of you.

VALENTINE'S DAY

* Happy Valentine's Day to YOU!

* I love you with all my heart. Happy Valentine's Day!

* Happy Hearts Day and a Million Happy Tomorrows. Happy Valentine's Day.

* With love to you on Valentine's Day.

* You are the ultimate Valentine!

* Thinking about you today and always. Happy Valentine's Day.

* Be Mine! Happy Valentine's Day.

* Thoughts of love to you today. Happy Valentine's Day.

* Hope your Valentine's Day is as sweet as they come….. and then some!

* I Love YOU. Happy Valentine's Day!

* You are the kind of person who's always remembered with love. Happy Valentine's Day

* I love you to infinity plus ONE! Happy Valentine's Day.

* You are the Best! Happy Valentine's Day.

* These days anyone can become anyone they want. Thank you for becoming my wife first! Happy Valentine's Day.

* For my husband with all my love for everything you do, for all we've shared for all the special things you are to me. Happy Valentine's Day.

* Please Be my Valentine!

* Do what makes you happy; Be with those who warm your hearts, Surround Yourselves with Love, for all the happiness you give to others all year long, Happy Valentine's Day!

*   There are precious few gems like you! Happy Valentine's Day.

*   You're the cinnamon on my toast! Happy "V" Day!

*   Happy Valentine's Day to a little sweetheart!

*   Te Amo, I Love You, WoAiNi, S'Agapo, JeT'aime. In any language, I LOVE YOU!

*   XOXOXOXOXO – Happy Valentines Day!

*   To my one and only, Happy Valentine's Day!

ABOUT THE AUTHOR

Ana Navarra has enjoyed arts and crafts since she can remember. She is a small business owner and a dog lover. Her passions in life are writing, reading and arts and crafts. She lives in Southern California with her husband and two dogs. She is currently working on building a multi-cultural online newsletter and writing a novel. She would love to hear from you! You can reach her at internationalbookstore@yahoo.com